Tony Hyland

An Essay Concerning the Fire and Passion of Paul Weller: His 50 Greatest songs

An Essay Concerning the Fire and Passion of Paul Weller: His 50 Greatest songs

By

Tony Hyland

A NEWINGTON PUBLICATION

About the author

Tony Hyland was born in East London, within the sound of the old Bow Bells, at Mile End Hospital, in November 1964.He has been a time served Career Civil Servant for most of his working career since leaving University of London and then Birkbeck College with a BA Hons in Political Science and an MSc in Politics and Sociology.

Tony's fiction and dramatizations flirt with a number of genre's especially Surrealism,Absurdism and the Theatre of Cruelty, but there is an underlying humour-mostly black it must be said-that is at the foundation of each the tales he tells-and is typical of his work.. There are incredible laugh out loud moments especially that will stop you in your tracks. There are also moments that will provoke you whether you like it or not.

Having already written an appreciation of one of his musical heroes, Randy Newman , he has moved to another, with this fascinating trawl through Paul Weller's back catalogue providing real insight and intelligence, having experienced 'close up' the emergence and dissolution of the Jam, the sophistication of the Style Council and the passion of his solo work. This is an unauthorised work of a real fan displaying a real enthusiasm for one of the great ongoing British musical careers.

Tony Hyland has also published the following plays and screen plays:

A Night at Sea
A Day in the Sun
The Interview
There's a party at my House Tonight!
What about Edu?
Fulham
A Woman's World
Monster of State
England Forever
Paris: A Novella

As well as 6 Volumes of Short Stories:

Phillip Mitchell celebrating the birthday of Soren Kierkegaard in Albert Square: Short stories Volume 1
The Transmogrification of Kenneth Barlow into John the Baptist on the cobbles of Coronation Street: Short stories Volume 2
Zak spoke Zarathustra: Short stories Volume 3
Waiting for Godot and/or Cliff Richard at Marylebone Station: Short Stories Volume 4
Detective Inspector Trident's Big Night Out: Short Stories Volume 5
Arthur Schopenhauer: First Alternative Stand-Up Comedian: Short Stories Volume 6

He has also published 'Randy Newman 12 Greatest Songs: An Appreciation'

Paul Weller: 50 Greatest Songs: Introduction by the Author:

I am just about to commit a cardinal sin and do one of the worst things any self-respecting writer can do and turn this introduction into a litany of apologies:

Apology number one : this is an unauthorized, albeit passionate view from one of Weller's most ardent fan's; a very personal view from those chaotic Jam gigs at the likes of the Marquee, the Rainbow and Hammersmith, which are still some of the highlights in my life, through to the recent tumultuous solo concerts celebrating his extraordinary creative resurgence and reacquaintance with his muse ; while this is also a very personal perspective of the songs that mean the most to me, not necessarily those most people regard as classics, but those which have somehow shaped my life, so apology number two goes to the majority of you that will no doubt carp at some of my entries and wish to conjure your own best-of- lists. Weller has such an impressive body of work I could have easily made this the 200 greatest Weller songs.

Apology number three relates to the preponderance of Jam tracks : once again they were 'my' band, and as a teenage boy ,learning about the world and maturing(about the 'young ideal' no less), many of those songs were so formative and life affirming for me ,and I know a number of you will empathise and will have lived through them with me .I love the Style Council and his solo work but for me the Jam remain one of the greatest of British bands and the songs endure and remain as potent as ever so hopefully you'll forgive me my passion for Weller's early triumphs.

In short, I've tried to distil the essence of Weller and how his songs have not only shaped my world but been indicative of our times, especially the depression and rancour of the late 70s and early 80s,so much so in fact that Weller has always retained a credibility with musical audiences, never having 'sold out', and never having abandoned his ambitions in challenging himself musically as well as remaining authentic-he is one of the only artists I can think of –Bowie likewise-who has managed this so successfully and with great conviction.

I do hope you enjoy this trawl through Weller's back pages, and this journey simultaneously forces you back to listening to some of the greatest songs that have emerged from one of our greatest songwriters.

Tony Hyland

October 2016

1: The Eton Rifles

I recall that frisson of excitement and pleasure listening to the 'Eton Rifles' for the first time on a John Peel session late into the night ,as it crashed and charged portentously as Weller hurled invective spitefully through the airwaves at the upper classes-a spectacularly powerful indictment of the class system-the preoccupation of Weller at the time, and a glorious set of lyrics that welded perfectly with the almost Wagnerian orchestration that so encapsulated the class war in an almost perfect top ten 45,a continuation of the startling run of magnificent singles that began with the masterpiece 'Down in the Tube Station at Midnight'.

Inspired by the sight of the unemployed marchers from Liverpool who were openly jeered by the Uppity upper classes on their way past Eton, Weller presciently captured what would be the ravages of Thatcherism, and of course, in a delicious slice of irony, David Cameron claimed it for himself as one of his favourite records, making it all the more remarkable. Surely he must understand, Weller has mused often in the recent past.

To my ears the song also captures the Jam as a formidably tight musical unit: Foxton's bass menacingly prominent throughout, while Buckler's drums providing the propulsion, supporting the force of the lyrics and the passion of Weller's vocals.

One of the greatest songs in the Jam's canon and arguably one of the greatest British 45's ever released.

'...Sup up your beer and collect your fags,
There's a row going on down near slough,
Get out your mat and pray to the west,

I'll get out mine and pray for myself.

Thought you were smart when you took them on,
But you didn't take a peep in their artillery room,
All that rugby puts hairs on your chest,
What chance have you got against a tie and a crest?

Hello-hurrah, what a nice day, for the Eton rifles,
Hello-hurrah, I hope rain stops play, with the Eton rifles.

Thought you were clever when you lit the fuse,
Tore down the House of Commons in your brand new shoes,
Compose a revolutionary symphony,
Then went to bed with a charming young thing.

Hello-hurrah, cheers then mate, it's the Eton rifles,
Hello-hurrah, an extremist scrape, with the Eton rifles.

What a catalyst you turned out to be,
Loaded the guns then you run off home for your tea,
Left me standing, like a guilty (naughty) schoolboy.

We came out of it naturally the worst,
Beaten and bloody and I was sick down my shirt,
We were no match for their untamed wit,
Though some of the lads said they'll be back next week.

Hello-hurrah, there's a price to pay, to the Eton rifles,
Hello-hurrah, I'd prefer the plague, to the Eton rifles.
Hello-hurrah, there's a price to pay, to the Eton rifles,
Hello-hurrah, I'd prefer the plague, to the Eton rifles...'

I remember the Jam appearance on 'Something Else' in 1979 playing this and
inspiring me to rebel too-it almost certainly helped me crystallize my thoughts about
society and the class system in general, and it also gave me an immense pride : this was
my band I had followed from the start in full force, majestically blowing the opposition
away.

It's all the more remarkable that such a young man proved so much in tune with his
muse and was able to encapsulate late seventies Britain so eloquently and thoughtfully.

2. Strange Town

On a recent evening out with a younger set; a motley crew of teenagers and twenty-somethings (no midlife crisis for me just a get together with some footie fans), I played the wonderful 'Strange Town' as an example of the contemporaneity of Weller and the Jam, and stunned them into silence as they paused, took breath, and ingested the sheer pop brilliance and force of this Jam masterpiece.

It's still amazing to think that this was realised at the start of 1979 on the back of the mighty 'Tube Station', heralding the glorious new Jam era and the remarkable surge in creative activity that saw them through to their demise.

I still find it stirringly powerful, 'aggressive'(very much of its time) as it literally erupts from its opening chords ; the wonderful chiming guitars, once again backed by the muscular backing of Foxton and Buckler, giving it a resonance still, and its tale of alienation and isolation in the big city remains timeless, a perfect encapsulation of the plight of many young people, finding themselves in a foreign environment, struggling for identity, struggling to cope with the disappointment of a promised land, that despite its promise of fame, fortune and adventure, inevitably lets you down.

Lyrically one of the best Weller Jam songs, capturing within this vignette a perfect depiction of the vicissitudes of life, and showing a depth and maturity way beyond Weller's years-it was clear his muse once again was flowing through him.

'...Found myself in a strange town
Though I've only been here for three weeks now
I've got blisters on my feet
Trying to find a friend in Oxford Street

I bought an A to Z guide book
Trying to find the clubs and YMCAs
But when you ask in a strange town
They say don't know, don't care
And I've got to go, mate

They worry themselves about feeling low
They worry themselves about the dreadful snow
They all ignore me 'cause they don't know
I'm really a spaceman from those UFOs

You've got to move in a straight line
You've got to walk and talk in four four time
You can't be weird in a strange town
You'll be betrayed by your accent and manners

You've got to wear the right clothes
Be careful not to pick or scratch your nose
You can't be nice in a strange town
Cause we don't know, don't care
And we got to go, man

Rush my money to the record shops
I stop off in a back street
Buy myself a snort
We got our own manifesto
Be kind to queers
And I'm so glad the revolution's here

It's nice and warm now!
I've finished with clubs where the music's loud
Cause I don't see a face in a single crowd
There's no one there

I look in the mirror
But I can't be seen
Just a thin, clean layer of mister sheen
Looking back at me
Oh, oh

Found myself in a strange town
Though I've only been here for three weeks now
I've got blisters on my feet
Trying to find a friend in Oxford Street
I bought an A to Z guide book
Trying to find the clubs and YMCAs
They say don't know, don't care
And I've got to go, mate

They worry themselves about feeling low
They worry themselves about the dreadful snow
They all ignore me 'cause they don't know
I'm really a spaceman from those UFOs

Strange town
Break it up
Burn it down, shake it up
Break it up…'

One of the great Jam singles.

3. When you're young

A perfect single which encapsulated the summer of 1979 for me –the renascent 'Mod' movement with the glorious Parkas, psychedelic paisley patterned shirts; the treks down Carnaby Street to get the latest Sta-Press or well-tailored suits, and of coursed those now cultish two-tone Jam shoes, all captured in this perfect indication of the Weller muse once again in full flow: one of the greatest songs ever written about the joy and ecstasy as well as the pain and anguish of just being young.

'…Life is timeless; days are long when you're young
You used to fall in love with everyone
Any guitar and any bass drum
Life is a drink and you get drunk when you're young

Life is new and there's things to be done
You can't wait to be grown up
Acceptance into the capital world
You pull on some weed, then you pull on someone when you're young

But you find out life isn't like that
It's so hard to comprehend
Why you set up your dreams to have them smashed in the end
But you don't mind you've got time on your side
And they're never gonna make you stand in line
You're just waiting for the right time

You're fearless and brave, you can't be stopped when you're young

You swear you're never ever gonna work for someone
No corporations for the new age sons
Tears of rage roll down your face
But still you say "it's fun"

And you find out life isn't like that
It's so hard to understand
Why the world is your oyster but your future's a clam
It's got you in its grip before your born
It's done with the use of a dice and a board
They let you think you're king but you're really a pawn

You're fearless and brave, you can't be stopped when you're young
You used to fall in love with everyone
Any guitar and any bass drum…'

The fiercely independent Weller streak appears again.

What's interesting is how Weller turns this into an anthem for contemporary Mods but also signifies his belief in the paramountcy of the individual struggling for identity against the masses-it's almost a hymn to existentialism too.

Musically a great melody which fizzes in the air, a real snap, crackle pop of a record that remains as joyful today as the first time I heard and adored it-magnificent !

4. Going Underground

It's been well documented that as the Jam were trying again fruitlessly and somewhat pointlessly to 'crack' America, whilst indeed in the deep south receiving the lukewarmist of reviews, news came through that this magnificent single had entered the British charts at number 1, which at the time was a remarkable achievement-something only the likes of Slade had achieved before-strange bedfellows indeed.

On the back of the breakthrough 'Eton Rifles', 'Going Underground' proved cataclysmic, fairly shattering the eardrums of the nation with an anti-Nuclear protest song, a 'state of the nation' tune no less, and I was almost in tears upon hearing once again how my band was blowing away the Punk/New Wave opposition.

Weller had found perfect subject matter for him; the angry young man had conjured savage imagery and sarcasm, invoking his best lyrics thus far with a great melody and soaring chorus to depict the ravages of the contemporary Thatcher era.

'...Some people might say my life is in a rut,
But I'm quite happy with what I got
People might say that I should strive for more,
But I'm so happy I can't see the point.
Something's happening here today
A show of strength with your boy's brigade and,
I'm so happy and you're so kind
You want more money - of course I don't mind
To buy nuclear textbooks for atomic crimes
And the public gets what the public wants

But I want nothing this society's got.
I'm going underground, (going underground)
Well the brass bands play and feet start to pound
Going underground, (going underground)
Well let the boys all sing and the boys all shout for tomorrow
Some people might get some pleasure out of hate
Me, I've enough already on my plate
People might need some tension to relax
[Me?] I'm too busy dodging between the flak
What you see is what you get
You've made your bed, you better lie in it
You choose your leaders and place your trust
As their lies wash you down and their promises rust
You'll see kidney machines replaced by rockets and guns
And the public wants what the public gets
But I don't get what this society wants
We talk and talk until my head explodes
I turn on the news and my body froze
The braying sheep on my TV screen
Make this boy shout, make this boy scream!
Going underground, I'm going underground!...'

I also wonder how much Weller was also referring to his need to retreat from this new found stardom; he himself has reflected on how ill prepared he was for the sudden glare of publicity, and the fame, fortune and he has always retained an earthiness, a working class ethic, and how much 'Going Underground' reflects this desire to retreat from this is interesting to contemplate-even subconsciously there remains an ambiguity about the lyrics.

A double A side with the wonderfully psychedelic and trippy 'Dreams of Children', this remains unquestionably the greatest Jam single and one of the greatest Modernist Pop records ever made, sitting fearlessly alongside Townshend's 'I can see for Miles' and Davies' 'Waterloo Sunset'.

5. The Changing Man

Perhaps one of the most overtly existential of Weller's songs, the' Changing Man' indicates his ever changing moods indeed as he heralds in a new age, once again rejecting his political public spokesman stance-one he never coveted anyway-and expresses his insecurities, his ambiguities in a song with a wonderful melody, chiming a la Beatles, Small Faces, the Move 45s of bygone days, and of course even referencing ELO.

Weller's writing becomes more introspective, philosophical during this period as he becomes more conscious of his individuality, more concerned with offering a personal critique of his peccadilloes and vicissitudes-this is almost a spiritual record albeit not an obvious one.

'... Is happiness real?
Or am I so jaded
I can't see or feel, like a man been tainted
Numbed by the effect, aware of the muse
Too in touch with myself, I light the fuse

I'm the changingman, built on shifting sands
I'm the changingman, waiting for the bang
As I light a bitter fuse

Time is on loan, only ours to borrow
What I can't be today, I can be tomorrow

And the more I see, the more I know
The more I know, the less I understand.

I'm the changingman, built on shifting sands
I'm the changingman, waiting for the bang
To light a bitter fuse

It's a bigger part
When our instincts act
A shot in the dark
A movement in black

And the more I see, the more I know
The more I know, the less I understand.

I'm the changingman, built on shifting sands
(I don't have a plan)
I'm the changingman, waiting for the bang
to light a bitter fuse…'

One of Weller's greatest live songs and almost becoming his signature tune-
unquestionably a Britpop classic too, fitting all too well with the mood of the 'Noughties'
and the sounds emerging from the Blur and Oasis bandwagons.

This also brought a tear to the eye to every original Jam fan as it seemed to pick up on the
'Sound Affects' period and also epitomising Mod music-as indeed it still does.

Check out the brilliant video as well as the You Tube extracts from concerts and Jools
Holland shows-always played with a typical Welleresque power, punch and panache.

6. To be Someone

I would be surprised to find out that this magnificent snippet from All Mod Cons isn't the favourite Jam track of the Britpoppers ,Albarn ,Anderson and the Gallaghers as it initially appears to highlight what is so alluring about the pop music field and its excitement, but then also catalogues the dangers and vices inherent within-it's almost a Punkish Ray Davies, as Weller clearly channels the songwriting savvy of the Kink with his storyboard technique, and eloquent lyricism, with the potency of the sound propelled forward by Weller's striking guitar chords, and Foxton and Buckler's reinspired rhythm section-in essence a real step forward for the Jam and the onset of that glorious 1978-1980 period and that remarkable succession of singles as well as the wonderful albums of that era.

Remarkably, Weller proved prescient again as he seemed to transplant himself thirty years later as he tackled and conquered the rock star excesses that had intermittently possessed him.

'...To be someone must be a wonderful thing
A famous footballer a rock singer
Or a big film star, yes I think I would like that

To be rich and have lots of fans
Have lots of girls to prove that I'm a man
And be no. 1 - and liked by everyone

Getting drugged up with my trendy friends
They really dig me and I dig them
And the bread I spend - is like my fame - it's quickly diminished

And there's no more swimming in a guitar shaped pool
No more reporters at my beck and call
No more cocaine its only ground chalk

No more taxis now we'll have to walk

But didn't we have a nice time
didn't we have a nice time?
Oh wasn't it such a fine time

I realize I should have stuck to my guns
Instead shit out to be one of the bastard sons
And lose myself - I know it was wrong - but its cost me a lot

And there's no more drinking after the club shuts down,
I'm out on me arse with the rest of the clowns
It's really frightening without a bodyguard
So I stay confined to my lonely room…'

Never has the Billy Liarish quest for an illusory fame been so astutely and wittily
observed and once again it seems remarkable that somebody so young could capture the
plight of fame and fortune and turn it into such a winning pastiche.

Very surprised that Weller hasn't made this a staple in his live shows in later years as it
seems to summarise the careers of a great many of his forebears and contemporaries, and
indeed himself, as he freely admitted, having conquered those demons.

A Jam classic from the classic Modernist album.

7. Going my way

No wonder Weller regards this as one of his greatest songs: a bona fide classic that exemplifies how he has mastered the song writing craft; try imagining any of the contemporary singers such as Adele, Sam Smith etc, and even going back to a soulful Amy Whitehouse wrapping those vocal cords around such a beautiful lyric and melody and you have an instant number one and certainly not an incongruous one.

Taken from the recent ,and wonderful, 'Saturn's Pattern', this is Weller's balladry at its best : a song appearing to be so simple but building into a modernist crescendo,doo wops included, and a neo soul groove underpinning it.

It reminds me of listening to a lot of Burt Bacharach's timeless classics that endure and can translate into any language, and interpretations from a multiplicity of singers and/or bands.

I can even hear a Dusty Springfield performing this on a 1967 special preparing for her 'Dusty in Memphis' period.

'...Into your heart
Into your heart, I'm running away
I wanna stay with you

You following me, am I following you?
I don't care anyway
As long as you stay with me

Many hearts were broke on the way
It gets hard to say
Smile a while at our lives yet unseen

It's the world at play

As if by chance, they could tell our fate
These tea leaf traces on empty plates

Sparkle and shine
Bird on the wing
Are you going my way?
Going my way with me

Play by my side
Stay with the beat
Are you going my way?
Going my way with me
With me

Many hearts were broke on the way
It gets hard to say
Smile a while at our lives yet unseen
It's the world at play

Wonder, oh wonder
Where will we go next?

Time slipping by
Time on the wind
Are you going my way?
Going my way with me

Am I following you, you following me?
I don't care anyway
As long as you stay... with me
With me

I'm so glad I found you now
Flying through the universe
Floating' on the sound around
Gone today but never gone

Flying through the universe
I'm so glad I found you now
Floating' on the sound around
Flying through the universe...'

Shamefully ignored on its release as a single-although simultaneously being proclaimed
as a Weller classic-this song will prove its longevity in later generations-and of course

stands as a contemporary Mod classic.

I've seen Weller perform this several times and he always seems lovingly entranced by it, and confident in singing what is clearly one of the best recent songs of our time.

Surely a place on a film soundtrack in the future will cement its place amongst rock classics.

Proper Mod!!!!

8. Boy about Town

Great to see Weller has recently revived this modernist classic from 'Sound Affects' in his live set; perhaps the greatest Mod single that never was from 1980, and brings about wonderful memories for me of the joy of that record and the period in general.

The Jam were at the height of their powers and of course 'Sound Affects' was their ultimate album and this delicious slice of pop brilliance typified for me the confidence that we fans had at our position, walking heads up, peacocks strutting up and down the streets : nights at the Rainbow, Finsbury Park; those nights at Hammersmith-the assurity that we supported THE best band, belonged to something important as indeed we did, dressed in the tailored garms our measly funds could afford (pure Quadrophenia !) from the Carnaby Street shops,cherished for sorties to Brighton or the West End, or indeed for our Concert nights.

'…See me walking around I'm the boy about town that you heard of
See me walking the streets I'm on top of the world that you heard

Oh like paper caught in wind
I glide up street, I glide down street
Oh and it won't let you go
Till you finally come to rest or someone picks you up
Up street down street and puts you in the bin

See me walking around I'm the boy about town that you heard of
See me walking the streets I'm on top of the world that you heard
Oh I'm sitting watching rainbows
And watching the people go crazy

Oh please leave me aside
I want to be a, I want to be,
I want to live in,
Up street down street like paper caught in wind
Up street down street it won't let you go

Na na na nah, na na na nah
Na na na na na na nah

Na na na nah, na na na nah
There's more than you can hope for in this world…'

I still trill these words on balmy summer evenings especially when things are going well, always seeing myself in a Who video from the 1960s, a la 'I'm the face'.

This song evidently sees Weller's muse bless him again with a great confidence and style-believing himself finally at writing things of the quality of his idols, McCartney, Lennon, Marriott and Davies-any of whom I could imagine being proud to sing a song of such quality.

9. Life from a Window

For me 'This is the Modern World' has always been criminally undervalued, dare I say, even by the Jam members themselves-Weller himself has acknowledged the pressures of being coerced into making the difficult second album at startling speed on the back of the momentous 'In the City'.

For any true Jam fan however, the album still represented a development and a greater depth in subject matter, and indeed it stands the test of time in the quality of Weller's writing, this track epitomising the growth in Weller's songwriting nous.

'Life from a Window' remains for many a fan one of Weller's great early songs, one which typifies the preoccupations of teenage years : isolation,introspection,innocence and vulnerability, themes Weller would go on to mine on subsequent albums and especially capture so beautifully on 'All Mod Cons' and 'Setting Sons'-indeed this was a band in transition, and Weller was learning his craft in public as it were and at such speed-amazing to think Weller was still a teenager, grappling with these issues and of course there was the great impact poetry had upon his writing, Adrian Henri,Roger Mcgough etc,and Weller was not afraid to lay himself open lyrically especially during the punk explosion which at the time was such a brave decision to make.

'...Looking from a hill top, watching from a lighthouse,
Just dreaming
Up here I can see the world,
Ooh, sometimes it don't look nice - that's OK

Life from a window, I'm just taking in the view
Life from a window, observing everything around you
Staring at a grey sky, try to paint it blue,
teenage blue

Some people that you see around you, tell you how devoted they are
They tell you something on Sunday, but come Monday they've changed their minds

I'm looking from a skyscraper
I'm standing on the Post Office tower
So I can see - all there is to see...'.

Weller took the sentiments of this song into his future compositions with great success and we should not underestimate the beauty and influence of this song.

I await the inevitable reappraisal of this and indeed the album it appeared on with bated breath.

It will happen. Wait and see.

Mark my words.

10. The Man in the Corner Shop

When I think of the late Nineteen Seventies in Britain I invariably recall the overwhelming and oppressive gloom of the Thatcher era so quickly following on from the rigours of what had preceded it : strikes, rubbish tips, shortened working weeks, and of course the class system as often personified by our soap operas, especially Coronation Street, and unless I am wildly off the mark this beauty from 'Sound Affects' must encapsulate those moments when Mike Baldwin ventured into Alf Robert's corner shop, purchasing his cigars and flaunting his wealth, while the locals struggled on.

One of Weller's greatest set of lyrics and story boards-pure Kinks circa 1967-capturing the age of inequality-a nascent Socialism and Humanism in his writing, although indeed the man in the corner shop becomes the everyman-it is nice to be your own boss really-pure Thatcherism itself and ironic given her upbringing as the daughter of a corner shop grocer.

'… Puts up the closed sign does the man in the corner shop
Serves his last and he says goodbye to him
He knows it is a hard life
But it's nice to be your own boss really

Walks off home does the last customer
He is jealous of the man in the corner shop
He is sick of working at the factory
Says it must be nice to be your own boss (really)

Sells cigars to the boss from the factory
He is jealous is the man in the corner shop
He is sick of struggling so hard
He says- it must be nice to own a factory

Go to church do the people from the area

All shapes and classes sit and pray together
For here they are all one
For God created all men equal…'.

The grind of working class life as envisioned by the man sick of working in the factory
wanting something more out of life-indeed how prescient this was of the 80s obsession
with the acquisition of wealth and the clarion call for people to rise above their station-in
fact a standard Wellerism of sticking out from the crown, swerving away from the
numbers but ultimately retaining a humanity and concern for people.

In essence a beautiful, yet thought provoking pop classic with a gorgeous melody-
timeless, once again something any of the greatest songwriters would be proud of.

It wouldn't be out of place on a 'Revolver' or a 'Something Else', or the Small Faces
'Ogden nut's flake'.

A truly great Weller song.

11. Down in the Tube Station at Midnight

Unarguably the first momentous Jam single, heralding the new era of glorious music and the efflorescence of Weller's writing .

Interestingly enough Vic Coppersmith Heaven recently recalled that Weller was on the verge of putting these lyrics in the wastebin, and was reluctantly persuaded to work with the band on the song ; Fox ton's bassline being a perfect foundation for the songs subject matter : a night out in the 1970s facing the oppression of the streets and clubs with the youth explosion happening, and that perilous ride home to your loved ones-people forget how there was an air of menace and aggression in the air during these times-and there did appear a prevalent anger and violence which Weller captures magnificently here.

Once again the Ray Davies influence is clear as Weller creates a perfect vignette, a play for today in fact, portraying the plight of the vulnerable man travelling into a modern nightmare if you like.

'...The distant echo
Of faraway voices boarding faraway trains
To take them home to
The ones that they love and who love them forever
The glazed, dirty steps repeat my own and reflect my thoughts
Cold and uninviting, partially naked
Except for toffee wrappers and this morning's paper
Mr. Jones got run down
Headlines of death and sorrow, they tell of tomorrow
Madmen on the rampage
And I'm down in the tube station at midnight
I fumble for change, and pull out the Queen
Smiling, beguiling
I put in the money and pull out a plum behind me
Whispers in the shadows, gruff blazing voices

Hating, waiting
"hey boy" they shout, "have you got any money?"
And I said, "I've a little money and a take away curry,
I'm on my way home to my wife.
She'll be lining up the cutlery,
You know she's expecting me
Polishing the glasses and pulling out the cork"
And I'm down in the tube station at midnight
I first felt a fist, and then a kick
I could now smell their breath
They smelt of pubs and wormwood scrubs
And too many right wing meetings
My life swam around me
It took a look and drowned me in its own existence
The smell of brown leather
It blended in with the weather
It filled my eyes, ears, nose and mouth
It blocked all my senses
Couldn't see, hear, speak any longer
And I'm down in the tube station at midnight
I said I was down in the tube station at midnight
The last thing that I saw
As I lay there on the floor
Was "Jesus saves" painted by an atheist nutter
And a British rail poster read "have an away day, a cheap holiday
Do it today!"
I glanced back on my life
And thought about my wife
Cause they took the keys, and she'll think it's me
And I'm down in the tube station at midnight
The wine will be flat and the curry's gone cold
I'm down in the tube station at midnight
Don't want to go down in a tube station at midnight...'

With this song Weller raised the bar and set the tone for the 'All Mod Cons' album and developed the third person form of writing which served him so well and allowed him to fully develop his style into the' Gift' Period.

It also has that timeless quality and was so often the highlight of the later Jam live shows heralding our journey into the dark night and into the very tube stations themselves-still not the safest of environments !

Bona fide Weller classic and one of his greatest lyrics. Thank god the lyric sheet didn't stay in the bin !!!

12 .Peacock Suit

Another Weller classic, rightfully acknowledged as a celebration of all things 'Mod', Weller cranks up the style and rocks out, extolling the virtues of the fashion obsessed fraternity for whom style is a way of life and an eternal obsession.

This sits comfortably with the 'Boy about Town' modernist sensibility and has become a live favourite.

One of the great solo Weller 45s which would sit comfortably on 'Sound Affects' and flourished in that era.

Weller has always disliked the social commentator's stance, being sceptical of the polemical, didactic songwriters who propose to offer solutions to the world's woes and this song summarises this antipathy all too well.

He has always pushed people to find their own solutions politically-in fact his distrust of all politicians has been a preoccupation of his for years.

'...I've got a grapefruit matter
It's as sour as shit
I have no solutions
Better get used to it

I don't need a ship to sail in stormy weather
I don't need you to ruffle the feathers - on my Peacock Suit

I'm Narcissus in a puddle
In shop windows I gloat
Like a ball of fleece lining
In my camel skin coat

I don't need a ship to sail in stormy weather
I don't need you to ruffle the feathers - on my Peacock Suit

Did you think I should
Nemesis in a muddle
In a mirror I look
In my rattlesnake shoes

I don't need a ship to sail in stormy weather
I don't need you to ruffle the feathers - of my Peacock Suit…'

The peacock in Weller stands proud through ; the rampant individualism of Mod too as well as the egoism and the hedonism-the Stevie Marriott ideal vision of Mod style, not needing anybody to ruffle the feathers of his peacock suit.

The cranking guitar lines, aggressively lurching us forward, displaying a militancy and power which he has honed to perfection in his live shows-the Wilkoisms abound once again-it would be amazing to see either Stevie Marriott or a Lee Brilleaux of Dr Feelgood getting their tonsils around this and either could do this classic slab of rock justice.

I'm in no way condescendingly calling this one of Weller's 'Pub Rock-Canvey Island' classics.

13. I Got By In Time

If we forget that the Jam first album 'In the City' was one of the first outpourings of the nascent punk/new wave movement which in a way gives it so much significance, and try to judge it neutrally and objectively, it is easy to see it as a joyous mesh of Sam and Dave and Iggy Pop-a pure rhythm and blues classic dipped in a dollop of Beatlesque songsmithery.

'I got by in time' is one of the most unheralded songs in the Jam canon and it is still remarkable to think how young Weller was when he penned this.

'…Saw a girl that I used to know
I was deep in thought at the time
To recognize the face at first
Cause I was probably looking at mine
Well she was the only girl I've ever loved
But my folks didn't dig her so much
I was young
This is serious
To me she was the world (she was my world now)
I thought I'd never live without her,
But I got by in time
Well let me tell you now,

Saw a guy that I used to know
Man he'd changed so much
I think it hurt him to say 'hello,
Cause he hardly opened his mouth
Yeah well he was my best friend a few years ago
Truly inseparable
We were young

We were full of ideals
We were gonna pull this whole world
But something happened
I didn't know why
But that's the way that it goes.

I suppose, What you say - what you do
Don't mean nothing, nothing at all
And all the bonds you make between ya
Can be broken any time you want now
Please tell me if my philosophy's wrong
I've got to know the truth
I don't mean to offend anyone but,
You know it's something that I do, oh-
So nice to see you tonight,
And I'm so glad that you came
Some of the people standing outside, say
Sure feel the same
Yeah my point is in a round about way
Given time he'll always forget
Cause the memories
That ... me on
To me everything (you're everything now)
And it always will be mine, yeah
And no one can take them away…'

Try to imagine an Otis Redding or Marvin Gaye singing this at their peak and you'll
understand what I mean.

Weller's lyrical obsessions, .i.e., the transience of youth, the relationships that can go
southwards very easily are neatly encapsulated here in a stunning R and B frenzy.

I remember the early Jam shows, marvelling at the power and style of Weller as he
pulverised through this song, and Foxton and Buckler rhythmically gave it a real
swagger.

It should never have been a real surprise to anybody that Weller would find refuge in
Soul and R and B after the demise of the Jam and want to explore more the music that he
really loved.

The sings were there for all to see as early as this early Weller Classic which to these ears
remains as fresh as the first time it sparkled on the first album and of course in the early
live shows.

14 .Mermaids

Mermaids represents Weller at his most effortless : a beautiful melody, a very simple love song-almost a summation of all the sounds of 1967 and the Mod, Pop sensibility at its finest.-and one song again you can playfully imagine being covered by a range of 60s pop groups through to current singers/bands : a timeless classic.

Taken from Paul's fourth solo album 'Heavy Soul' which was generally well received and remains one of the strongest singles from his solo collection and one of the choicest cuts from the album.

It's one of those melodies that must just come to him so easily as so many of his classics have done-let's think 'That's Entertainment' here for example, flowing out after a night in the local boozer.

'…She's in my head
She's in my mind
And I'm all she says
Yes she knows me well
As well as you can

She's on my side
I often hide
In her magic hair
And there I learn again, the joy of life
The wonder of it all
And this I feel, that through her I learn
Another way to be

You take my breath, I feel consumed

Take it all, I want to know
What lies behind, your smiles and shells
Wish I knew you well
Come in my head
Come in my mind
You can only love, when you open up
To be yourself…'

To me Weller is tapping here into his inner Townshend, Love and the Who circa 68/69, with the gorgeous tune and the poetic lyricism of the piece, but also possesses strains of the Stevie Winwood early period Traffic days-that irresistible combination of whimsy and melody that was so indicative of Mod at its height.

Woefully unregarded and not often aired live it's surely not long before a critical re-evaluation sees this elevated to the list of Weller classics.

Effortless pop brilliance.

15. No Tears to Cry

There has been no doubt as to Wellers brilliance and songsmithery but it was remarkable how many people including a great many friends of mine did not believe that this track was a Weller original, thinking it was a Bacharach classic from a bygone age, ripe for on a Dusty Springfield version or even more contemporaneously by the sadly deceased Amy Whitehouse.

A powerhouse of a song that is timeless and destined to be covered by an Adele or a Sam Smith-I'm not being derogatory here; both singers have great voices that could do justice to this song.

'...If you don't want to see me fall
Turn your face to the wall
There's no place left to hide
There's no tears to cry
'cos my eyes have dried
If you can't see my wanting from afar
Can't you see how distant We are
There's no way I can lie
There's no tears to cry
'cos my eyes have dried

Time before the thief
Who stole a precious mind
Wrapped it up in silk
And sold it to the night
If you don't want to watch
watch me slide
Turn around here inside
Find a place we can hide
There's no tears to cry

There's no place left inside
There's no tears to cry
'cos my eyes have dried
There's no tears to cry…'

What was most jarring was how this appeared in the midst of the current Weller renaissance and the creative period that has spawned such creativity a la Bowie, Neu, Can and even Eno, whilst he still retained that knack for a beautiful melody and lyrical solipsism (sophistication?): this seems to come out of nowhere as if he were channelling the Bacharach and Jerry Wexler within him to write something that would have sat snugly on 'Dusty in Memphis'.

A remarkable song and one of his greatest homages to the 60s torch song a la Scott Walker et al.

I warmly await vindication as to when an Adele or Sam Smith send this into the stratosphere!

16. Come on , Let's go

Part of the evolutionary process for any artist must be a reacquaintance with his or her past, and evaluation of previous works in order to move on.

'Come on, Let's go' has the feel of a Weller looking to find the effervescence of the early R and B fuelled Jam period, as it recreates the world of the Feelgoods,the early Who and a modern soul to produce another pop classic.

Culled from the 'As is Now' set it's a lively reminder of the brilliance of Weller in condensing a range of images into a powerful aggressive guitar based Wilko influenced romp.

'...You have never been there
Till you've heard the fat girl sing
Then nothing else matters
Everything just pales with in
Hanging round the corners
Shouting at the top of your voice
Sing you little fuckers
Sing like you got no choice
I believe it's true
We are everywhere
And I feel the wind
And it feels so high
There really is no purpose
Definitely is no need
To go running round the houses
Like a racehorse on speed
[Chorus:]
I believe again

We are everything
And I feel the wind
And it gets so high
Come on
Baby let's go
Oh come on
Baby let's go
You say where to
I say I don't know
I just need to run
And you need it too
And I catch your eye
And I feel the wind
And it feels so high
We're planting up the acorns
Wondering to where they'll lead
We're planting up the acorns
Wondering to where they'll seed
[Chorus]
You say where to
I say I don't know…'

It's surely also the brother record to 'From the Floorboards up', and sets the scene for the
rockier,rootsier phase of his solo career, before the meshing of styles that emerged from
'22 Dreams' onwards.

The song also possesses a fine melody and once again is a fine example of Weller's
ability to retain the songsmithery gold standard even with what appears to be a
rudimental riff ; its' as if Weller has such good habits when writing that he just can't help
himself but come up with songs of such quality when it appears he's not even trying –a
rare talent indeed ,only possessed by the great songwriters.

17. Sunflower

If 'Into Tomorrow' heralded the start of Weller's prolific and productive solo career, then 'Sunflower' represented for many the first post Jam record that would almost be the template for his later work.

Weller once again channels the Small Faces 'Tin Soldier' era with a dose of classic Winwood infused Traffic and then throws in, some may say, a tinge of Neil Young, who certainly proved to be an influence over time-I cite Weller's blistering cover of the wonderful 'Ohio' as evidence of this.

Lyrically we see Weller's preoccupations once again become very insular; the introspection of Weller's solo career at the forefront, as well as a scepticism and cynicism taking over, and there is a certain rejoicing in the fact that he is very much in control, doing his own thing, finding his muse once again after the dissolution of the Style Council and the difficult post period exploring and re-engaging with his roots as typified by the first Weller solo record.

'...don't care how long this lasts
We have no future - we have no past
I write this now while I'm in control
I'll choose the words and how the melody goes
Along winding streets, we walked hand in hand
And how I long for that sharp wind
To take my breath away again
I'd run my fingers through your hair
Hair like a wheat field, I'd run through
That I'd run through
And I miss you so I miss you so
No you're gone, I feel so alone
I miss you so
I'd send you a flower a sunflower bright

While you cloud my days, messing up my nights
And all the way up to the top of your head
Sunshower kisses, I felt we had
And I miss you so I miss you so
All I gotta do, is think of you and I miss you so…'

Often a live favourite, it's Weller at his most authentic I feel, giving full range to the melodious side of his music, the rockier Modfather, and producing a renewed lyrical depth.

Certainly one of the Weller classics that will stand the test of time.

18. You do something to me

As Weller himself has noted, it was around the 'All Mod Cons' era that he became less self-conscious re penning explicit love songs a la 'English Rose' and 'It's too bad'-this of course was something he was to experiment more in the Style Council especially with the Cappuccino Kid coming up with a whole medley of classic love songs, which has culminated in some stunning ballads in his solo career which of course is exemplified in this new standard classic from the 'Stanley Road' set.

A beautiful song which has graced films, TV shows and has become dare I say his signature tune for many fans-many of whom have used it as 'their' song, and one can imagine as with so many of his classic moments, a whole array of contemporary or past singers having a stab at making it their own.

Using the usual Wellerian imagery of fire, passion and inspiration married with a gorgeous melody propelled by a beautiful piano riff which Weller has mastered a la Bacharach and the classics-think 'Going my Way' for example.

'...You do something to me
Something deep inside
I'm hanging on the wire
For a love I'll never find
You do something wonderful
Then chase it all away
Mixing my emotions
That throws me back again
Hanging on the wire,
I'm waiting for the change
I'm dancing through the fire,
Just to catch a flame
An' feel real again
Hanging on the wire,

Said I'm waiting for the change
I'm dancing through the fire,
Just to catch a flame
An' feel real again
You do something to me
Somewhere deep inside
I'm hoping to get close to
A peace I cannot find
Dancing through the fire yeah
Just to catch a flame
Just to get close to,
Just close enough
You do something to me - something deep inside…'

This sits as one of the true Weller classics.

19. Into Tomorrow

That period between the end of the Style Council and the struggles to find himself once again for his incipient solo career has been denoted as one of Weller's most difficult periods, similar to the backlash of the 'Modern World' and the writing block before the efflorescence of 'All Mod Cons', and no better statement of what was to come was the emergence of 'Into Tomorrow'; the rock groove a la the Jam and indeed pure Mod, unleashed with a lyrical imagery regarding his search for authenticity, a renewal of his flame praying that his time was not lost.

'...Into the mists of time and space
Where we have no say over date and place
Don't get embarrassed if it happens a lot,
That you don't know how you started or where you're gonna stop
And if at times it seems insane, all the tears in searching;
Turning all your joy to pain, in pursuit of learning;
Buy a dream and hideaway, can't escape the sorrow;
Your mojo will have no effect, as we head into tomorrow
Round and round like a twisted wheel
Spinning in attempt to find the feel
Find the path that will help us find
A feeling of control over lives and minds
And if at times it seems insane, all the tears in searching;
Turning all your joy to pain, in pursuit of learning;
Buy a dream and hideaway, can't escape the sorrow;
Your mojo will have no effect, as we head
Into the stars and always up
Drinking from a broken cup
Whose golden gleam is fading fast
Praying that it has not passed
Into tomorrow...'

Interesting that this track also sits snugly with the emergence of Britpop, being so redolent of his and Blur/Oasis influences, especially the Small Faces, the Kinks, even Traffic.

A standard live favourite and something that always summarises Weller's stance even up to current day-striving for the next challenge, combatting uncertainty, and musically not only remaining current and vibrant but in many cases setting the agenda.

20. In the City

It was very evident to anybody witnessing those first Jam shows and the residency at the Cow in London before the signing of their Polydor Record contract that the Jams first single had to be their standout track and their blistering paean to the joy of youth and the dreams of a young man intent on leaving the suburban sprawl of Woking and living out the pleasures and succumbing to the temptations of our beautiful capital city.

Weller has always spoken openly of his alienation especially in the early days in relation to his standing in the nascent punk community-the Metropolitan's Strummer,Lydon,Vicious etcetera who luxuriated in the confines of the London cliques that emerged late 76,early 77.

This wonderful opening Jam single expressed Weller's aspiration to discover himself in the London Streets he is now so familiar with and be a focal part of the youth movement that was formulating around him-interestingly Weller being pointedly younger than nearly all his contemporaries, and in effect being the real McCoy-the young ideal.

'...In the city there's a thousand things I want to say to you
But whenever I approach you, you make me look a fool
I wanna say, I wanna tell you
About the young ideas
But you turn them into fears
In the city there's a thousand faces all shining bright
And those golden faces are under 25
They wanna say, they gonna tell ya
About the young idea
You better listen now you've said your bit-a

And I know what you're thinking
You're sick of that kind of crap

But you'd better listen man
Because the kids know where it's at

In the city there's a thousand men in uniforms
and I've heard they now have the right to kill a man
we wanna say, we gonna tell ya
about the young idea
and if it don't work, at least we still tried

In the city, in the city
in the city there's a thousand things I want to say to you…'

Weller would continue to talk about and extol the 'young idea' and say a thousand things about the joys,temptations,excitement and indeed the precipitous learning curve that all young people endure to hopefully come out the other side as wise, productive human beings.

One of the greatest debut singles released and still serves as a remarkable indication of the imagery within Weller's lyricism, and of course the power of the Jam as a trio-a glorious introduction to the Woking wonders, no less.

21. All around the World

One of the most under-rated songs in the Jam canon, largely due to it not being featured on an album, but certainly one of the great early singles, of great quality ; a fizz bomb of a track that fully exploded in the wake of the 'In the City' debut 45.

For many Jam fans this represents indeed the start of the 'Modern World' itself.

Weller's preoccupation with Townshend and the Who's modernism were more than apparent here as he exhorts the young to find a new direction and a positive reaction-the antithesis of punk; what is the point of saying destroy unless you are a nihilist or an anarchist....Absolutely.

This is more a reaction to the punkish nihilism that was becoming all too fashionable particularly in the Cities of England where a violent reaction to the rank conservatism of the age and the banality of much of popular culture was taking place.

'...Oi!
All over the country
(We want a new direction)
I said all over this land
(We need a reaction)
Well there should be a youth explosion
(Inflate creation)
But something we can command
What's the point in saying destroy
I want a new life for everywhere
We want a direction
(All over the country)
I want a direction

(All over this land)
Because this is your last chance
You can't dismiss what is gone before
But there's foundations for us to explore
I said
All around the world I've been looking for new
Youth explosion!
A new direction
We want a reaction
Inflate creation
Looking for new!...'

Weller, once again 'away from the numbers', standing out from the crowd, advocating a new positivity. A need to push forward and engage positively-engaging the young idea no less ; certainly his clumsy flirtation with Conservatism was an expression more with his desire to change positively and cling onto the things that make, for many, Britain great-the 'Village Green Preservation Society' no less.

Naïve yes, but this was an eighteen year old finding his political identity in public and very much in the glare of the spotlight-and in a way this can be seen as a precursor to the politically more sophisticate and certainly more humanistic/socialistic 'wall's come tumbling down', the Style Council classic in later years.

Musically this is the Jam at their best-a tight R and B trio rocking out angst and urban ennui to an incredibly intense groove-a real powerhouse of a song live and yes remarkably underrated-certainly a great Jam single.

22. I Need You

The most unappreciated Jam album most certainly remains 'The Modern World' but for most Weller aficionados it exists as an important record as it plays its role as the transitional record from the youthful exuberance of 'in the City' to the establishment of Weller's song writing credentials on All mod cons, including many hints of the great things to come.

'I need you' plays on the influence of the Who and especially the Kinks introducing the balladry into Weller's writing which would flourish in later years.

'...I need you to keep me straight
When the world don't seem so great,
And it's hard enough you know

I need you to be around
When my conscience brings me down
And the world seems so obscure

I want you to be the one
Who tells me off when I do wrong,
And you know I can be bad
I need you, I need you
Say you'll stay, make my day

Now what have I done,
Was it something I said - oh dear

I need you to turn me off,

When you think I've said enough,
To the extent of being a bore
I need you to tell me no
Slap my wrists and send me home
Tell me I can't come again

Now why are you crying
Have I gone too far – again

I need you keep me straight,
when the world don't seem so great
and it's hard enough you know
I need you, I need you
Say you'll stay
Make my day…'

It seemed so out of step with the aggressive sounds emanating from the Punk/New Wave scene of that era but Weller, always being his own man, made clear his debt to the melodic sounds of the 1960s with this largely ignored Jam cut which melodically and lyrically has stood the test of time and I think could sit nicely in any Weller solo set of latter years.

It neatly paves the way for the later ballads and introduces a vulnerability in his writing which he has cultivated to great effect ever since.

This is the sound of a young man growing up and negotiating the emotional turmoil's of youth and relationships-a great Jam song and important in many ways demonstrating Weller's courage in his writing and staying true to his ideals.

23. Tonight at Noon

Weller has always had a strong poetic sensibility and for many of us he led us into the fields of literature and poetry and signposted the works of art important to any good Modernist-the poetry of the Beats,Orwell,Shelley etcetera and he played a pivotal part in the educational development of many a fan.

This undervalued classic from the 'Modern World' once again indicates Weller's bravery in going very much against the grain and writing beautiful love poetry encased in a beautiful melody-quite why this has been largely ignored by fans once again proves mystifying-but against the backdrop of 1977 and punk explosion it did appear so incongruous.

'...Tonight at noon, tonight at noon
When we meet in the midnight hour,
I will bring you night flowers (coloured)
Like your eyes

Tonight at noon, I'll touch your hand
Held for a moment amongst strangers
Amongst the dripping trees
Country girl

Walking in city squares in winter rain
Walking down muddy lanes or empty streets
Arranging a time and place to meet

Tonight at noon, you'll feel my warmth
You'll feel my body inside you
We'll be together for hours

Time and tears
Won't wait for evermore
For the time is now
And now is the time to explore
Why waste the world outside
When you're sure…'

Once again this paved the way for the beauty and power of much of the writing on 'All Mod Cons' and saw Weller flex his muscles with balladry, which he has certainly mastered-look at 'Going my Way' for example-a perfect ballad.

To these ears 'Tonight at Noon' is a song waiting to be covered and turned into a huge hit-the quality of the song writing is evident but as we have already noted both the album it came from and this song seemed so out of place given it was in the word of the Clash '1977'.

A great Weller song nonetheless.

24. English Rose

Somewhat mysteriously hidden away from the track listing of 'All Mod Cons',' English Rose' remains one of the greatest Weller Jam songs, and once again displays not only the versatility of his writing but also the fact that he was looking to hone his skills writing sublime ballads that have punctuated his work throughout the years.

To me the debt to Townshend in particular is evident here too, as well as the modernistic paean to love in the form of a young man's beautiful tribute to his English Rose-no one else compares- no one tempts me from she…

'…No matter where I roam
I will come back to my English rose
For no bonds can ever tempt me from she
I've sailed the seven seas,
Flown the whole blue sky.
But I've returned with haste
To where my love does lie.

No matter where I go
I will come back to my English Rose
For nothing can ever tempt me from she.
I've searched the secret mists,
I've climbed the highest peaks
Caught the wild wind home
To hear her soft voice speak
No matter where I roam
I will come back to my English Rose
For no bonds can ever tempt me from she.

I've been to ancient worlds
I've scoured the whole universe
And caught the first train home
To be at her side.

No matter where I go
I will return to my English Rose
For no bonds, nothing and no-one can ever keep me from she...'

There are also hints of McCartney in the imagery and of course the sublime melody and its ethereal quality-maybe it's hidden as it does seem to ghost into the 'All mod cons' set but ironically for that seems to fit so well-if the album represents a view of young people growing and evolving with time.

It remains a perfect Mod record existing perfectly in the modernist landscape.

Once again another Weller classic destined to be a hit for somebody else-Sam Smith? Ed Sheeran? Olly Murs?

Not as far-fetched as you think?

25. Away from the Numbers

One of the contradictions re Paul Weller and his standing in the songwriters pantheon as well as the moniker of the mod father is the fact that he has always been a private individual and if anything has always shied away from being the spokesman of a generation, the tag gifted him certainly after the glorious Sound Affects/Going Underground triumphs-and in essence 'Away from the Numbers' is perhaps the quintessential Weller song and I have never seen him play it with anything less than 100% commitment and energy-a passionate conviction.

Culled from the' In the City' set and a live favourite of many years (in fact a constant between 77-79) it's remarkably mod in style,melody,yet almost existential in its lyricism, glorifying solitude, tranquillity-a stance away from the norm, becoming a true individual and in a way finding oneself.

'...Things are getting just too cozy for me
And I see people as they see me
Gonna break away and gain control
You free your mind
You free your soul
I was the type who knocked at old men
(history's easy)
Who together at tables sit and drink beer
(somewhere is really)
Then I saw that I was really the same
So this link's breaking away from the chain
Away from the numbers
Away from the numbers
Is where I'm gonna be
Away from the numbers

Away from the numbers
Is where I am free
I was sick and tired of my little niche
Well gonna break away and find where life is
And all those fools I thought were my friends
(coaching is easy)
They now stare at me and don't see a thing
(reality's so hard)
Till their life is over and they start to moan
How they never had the chance to make good
Away from the numbers
Away from the numbers
Is where I'm gonna be
Away from the numbers
(away from the numbers)
Away from the numbers
Is where I am free
Is where I am free
Is where I'm gonna be
Is reality
Reality's so hard, reality's so hard…'

Certainly not an 'I'm in with the in crowd' sentiment or a song celebrating the tribalism that modernists advocated-being a part of a special fraternity, elite as it were.

One of the most enduring Jam sings and remarkable how Weller being so young was able to express so well the alienation-and desire for self-realization of youth, and was a portent to the more overt introspective solo classics that were to follow.

26. In the Crowd

One of the great characteristics of Weller throughout the years has been his Britishness and his unwillingness to dilute this in any way-in fact this has been a consistent critique of his work in his inability to move from a cult legend in the U.K to a major international star-not that Weller has ever seemed concerned by this much to his credit.

'In the Crowd' from 'All Mod Cons' is the quintessential example of Weller's Anglophilia,and his lyrical fascination with individualism; and being stifled at the hands of the Crowd, the mob, and the desire to escape the mundaneity of life.-he glorifies the baked beans on toast, the walls ice cream-memories for yours truly-we live within an age of conformity but for Weller there is also a security there, a simultaneous yearning for a freedom and a realization of all the aspirations that often get watered down or simply destroyed.

'...When I'm in the crowd, I don't see anything
My mind goes a blank, in the humid sunshine
when I'm in the crowd I don't see anything
I fall into a trance, at the supermarket
the noise flows me along, as I catch falling cans
of baked beans on toast, technology is the most.
and everyone seems just like me,
they struggle hard to set themselves free
and they're waiting for the change
When I'm in the crowd, I can't remember my name
and my only link is a pint of Wall's ice cream
when I'm in the crowd - I don't see anything
Sometimes I think that it's a plot,
an equilibrium melting pot
The government sponsors underhand

When I'm in the crowd
When I'm in the crowd
When I'm in the crowd
And everyone seems that they're acting a dream
cause they're just not thinking about each other
and they're taking orders, which are media spawned
and they should know better, now you have been warned
and don't forget you saw it here first
When I'm in the crowd
When I'm in the crowd
When I'm in the crowd
And life just simply moves along
in simple houses, simple jobs
and no one's wanting for the change
When I'm in the crowd
When I'm in the crowd
When I'm in the crowd…'

Musically one of the great Jam records-one of the first early songs that hinted at the landscapes that would be fully realized on 'Setting Sons' onwards and 'Sound Affects' in particular.

Always a live favourite and one Weller has revisited in latter years to great effect.

Another modern classic.

27. It's too Bad

'All Mod Cons' marks a watershed in the Jams career as we have already noted, and includes a number of tracks which encapsulate perfectly Wellers song writing preoccupations and lay bare the Beatlesque,Kinksian influences and there is no better template than the wonderful 'It's too Bad', which has the tinge of Lennon/McCartney with a beautiful melody and an effective but simple lyric which also demonstrates Weller's confidence in writing straightforward love songs much against the grain of the punk/new wave aggression of the period.

'…All we seem to do is talk about it
We always end up shouting about it
There was a time we could overcome it
But it's too late to say we'll just forget it
It's too bad that we had to break up
And too much said for us to every make up
I could get by if I could just forget you
But things remind me and I feel so sad now
I could say I'm sorry
But it's not the point is it?
You want to play your games and
You don't mind if I get hurt
Same old feeling every time I see you
And every avenue I walk I'm behind you
Your back is turned and your eyes are closed girl
You move in circles that are out of my reach now…'

It remained a constant live favourite for the Jam and saw the threepiece really show their mettle and how tight they were as a musical tour de force.

A tale of young love indeed and for us spotty youth teenagers it represented poetry of sorts-and had simplicity we could all relate to.

A beautiful song and an important one in the Weller canon.

28. A Bomb in Wardour Street

Even at the time of its release I was always perplexed by the double A sided 'David Watts/A Bomb in Wardour Street' –while David Watts was clearly an attempt to continue the run of consecutive hit singles with an admittedly workmanlike cover of the Kinks classic from 'Something Else' which hogged the airplay, it was 'A Bomb' that really excited and captured the imagination as it seemed to be heralding in a new era which of course' All Mod Cons' delivered with a Modernist bow and arrow.

'…Where the streets are paved with blood
With cataclysmic overtones
Fear and hate linger in the air
A strictly no-go deadly zone
I don't know what I'm doing here
'Cause it's not my scene at all
There's an 'A' bomb in Wardour Street
They've called in the Army, they've called in the police to
I'm stranded on the vortex floor
My head's been kicked in and blood's started to pour
Through the haze I can see my girl
Fifteen geezers got her pinned to the door
I try to reach her but fall back to the floor
'A' bomb in Wardour Street
It's blown up the West End, now it's spreading throughout the City
'A' bomb in Wardour Street, it's blown up the City
Now it's spreading through the country
Law and order take a turn for the worst
In the shape of a size 10 boot
Rape and murder throughout the land
And they tell you that you're still a free man

If this is freedom I don't understand
'Cause it seems like madness to me
'A' bomb in Wardour Street, Hate Bomb
Hate Bomb, Hate Bomb, Hate Bomb
A Philistine nation, of degradation
And hate and war. There must be more
It's Doctor Martin's A,P,O,C,A,L,Y,P,S,E,
Apocalypse!...'

Weller captured so brilliantly the aggression of the time and the dangers lurking around the streets of the London especially the West End at that time ;having been mugged on Wardour Street on the way to the Marquee at the time it was all too lucid to me-and the power chords and riff thundered home the point in one of the great, largely overlooked, Jam classics.

To me at the time it was redolent of the Clash as well as a throwback to the glories of the early Who ; it has stood the test of time and still sounds as potent as it was on its release.

One of the great Weller lyric sheets too as he became more ambitious in chronicling the sights and sounds of our time which he would take to further levels of greatness with 'Tube Station', 'Eton Rifles', 'That's Entertainment'-but this is a precursor to these masterpieces, make no mistake.

29. Thick as Thieves

Wellers writing reached new heights with the 'Setting Sons' set and lyrically 'Thick as Thieves' is as good as any song Paul Weller has written-it's no surprise as it appears to be one of his favourites and for me it has a particular resonance as I lived and breathed it from its first hearing on the album-it's a wonderful song about the fleeting nature of friendship and being young especially, yet it remains a classic and could feature seamlessly in his current live set of latter years.

It's easy to see why this song resonates so easily with young people and mods find its captivating-it could have been a cornerstone on Quadrophenia-and indeed I'll controversially claim Weller as a better lyricist than Townshend-I'm not denigrating Townshend but he's never written a lyric this good !

'...Times were so tough, but not as tough as they are now,
We were so close and nothing came between us, and the world,
No personal situations.
Thick as thieves us, wed stick together for all time,
And we meant it but it turns out just for a while,
We stole, the friendship that bound us together
We stole from the schools and their libraries,
We stole from the drugs that sent us to sleep,
We stole from the drink that made us sick,
We stole anything that we couldn't keep,
And it was enough, we didn't have to spoil anything,
And always be as thick as thieves.
Like a perfect stranger, you came into my life,
Then like the perfect lone ranger, you rode away, rode away,
Rode away, rode away.
We stole the love from young girls in ivory towers,

We stole autumn leaves and summer showers,
We stole the silent wind that says you are free,
We stole everything that we could see,
But it wasn't enough, and now we've gone and spoiled everything,
Now were no longer as thick as thieves.
You came into my life,
Then like a perfect stranger you walked away, walked away,
Walked away, walked away.
Thick as thieves us, wed stick together for all time,
And we meant it but it turns out just for a while,
We stole the friendship that bound us together.
We stole the burning sun in the open sky,
We stole the twinkling stars in the black night,
We stole the green belt fields that made us believe,
We stole everything that we could see.
But something came along that changed our minds,
I don't know what and I don't know why,
But we seemed to grow up in a flash of time,
While we watched our ideals helplessly unwind.
No, were no longer as thick as thieves, no,...'

Musically a triumph too for three piece and always incredibly powerful live-words spat
out with always a passion and inspiration.

This song makes you proud to be a Jam fan in so many ways and has stood the test of
time.

30. Private Hell

'Private Hell' is another watershed moment in Paul Weller's writing : there is a great sophistication in the lyrical imagery and real poetic knowing in the verse while it still retains the passion and fervency of the Jam at full force.

As with the other great songwriters at the height of their powers (Lennon,McCartney,Davies,Bowie especially) he's now able to encapsulate a screenplay, a veritable play for today, prevalent of any time and still contemporaneous, into a 3 minute pop magnum opus highlighting the fatuities of family and modern life in general.

'...Closer than close, you see yourself,
A mirrored image, of what you wanted to be.
As each day goes by, a little more,
You can't remember, what it was you wanted anyway.
The fingers feel the lines, they prod the space,
Your aging face, the face that once was so beautiful,
Is still there but unrecognizable,
Private hell.
The man who you once loved, is bald and fat,
And seldom in, working late as usual.
Your interest has waned, you feel the strain,
The bed springs snap, on the occasions he lies upon you,
Close your eyes and think of nothing but,
Private hell.
Think of Emma, wonder what she's doing,
Her husband terry, and your grandchildren.
Think of Edward, who's still at college,
You send him letters, which he doesn't acknowledge.
cause he don't care,

They don't care.
cause they're all going through their own - private hell.
The morning slips away, in a Valium haze,
And catalogues, and numerous cups of coffee.
In the afternoon, the weekly food,
Is put in bags, as you float off down the high street
The shop windows reflect, play a nameless host,
To a closet ghost, a picture of your fantasy,
A victim of your misery, and private hell
Alone at 6 o'clock, you drop a cup,
You see it smash, inside you crack,
You can't go on, but you sweep it up
Safe at last inside your private hell.
Sanity at last inside your private hell…'

For me this was poetry at its best in my teenage years and typified what Weller was to
later describe as his 'grapefruit matter'-as sour as shit,although its his realism, his ability
to empathise with young people and speak to our generation about the things that moved
and indeed troubled us that he managed with such power and conviction that has stood
the test of time.

One of the great Jam live songs too-always value the recorded live versions as they
capture the real passion and power as the band launch forward propelled by Weller's
fury.

Another Weller classic.

31. Wasteland

We have noted the transition Weller made from the vigour of the inflammatory' In the City', to the introspective pieces on 'This is the Modern World', and 'All Mod Cons' social commentary, and the sophistication of the lyrical context from 'Setting Sons' onwards-and perhaps 'Wasteland' is the song that best encapsulates the integration of these qualities best-one of the greatest Weller songs, the nod to T S Eliot's youthful evocations of his time (how this paints a picture of late seventies Britain and the plight of young people during this time).

'...Meet me on the wastelands - later this day
We'll sit and talk and hold hands maybe
For there's not much else to do in this drab and colourless place
We'll sit amongst the rubber tyres
Amongst the discarded bric-a-brac
People have no use for - amongst the smouldering embers of yesterday

And when or if the sun shines
Lighting our once beautiful features
We'll smile but only for seconds
For to be caught smiling is to acknowledge life
A brave but useless show of compassion
And that is forbidden in this drab and colourless world

Meet me on the wastelands - the ones behind
The old houses - the ones - left standing pre-war
The ones overshadowed by the monolith monstrosities
Councils call homes
And there amongst the shit - the dirty linen

The holy Coca-Cola tins - the punctured footballs
The ragged dolls - the rusting bicycles
We'll sit and probably hold hands
And watch the rain fall - watch it - watch it
Tumble and fall - tumble and falling
Like our lives - like our lives
Just like our lives

We'll talk about the old days
When the wasteland was release when we could play
And think - without feeling guilty
Meet me later but we'll have to hold hands
Tumble and fall - tumble and falling
Like our lives - like our lives
Exactly like our lives…'

Once again this track for me has such special significance; I was so impressed by
Weller's ability to conjure up images that were so striking, indicative of the time, but did
it so magically, beautifully in fact, with a depth that very few contemporary songwriters
could muster.

One of my favourites yes but I still dislike the quality of the recorded 'Setting Sons'
version-for me the beauty of the song struggles to emerge from a leaden, stodgy
production sound which buries the song but nonetheless this remains one of the greatest
Weller songs and still sounds timeless-meet me in the wasteland indeed-in this drab and
colourless place, forbidding passion, and light-but of course as Weller actually exhorts,
we must remain positive and find a way out.

32. Saturday's Kids

Settings sons was such a natural progression from the Modernist vignettes captured in 'All Mod Cons' and the wonderful 'Saturdays Kids' perfectly encapsulates Weller's preoccupations of the period: giving slice of life images of what it was like to be young during this period :'…drive Cortina's fur trimmed dash board-stains on the seats-in the back of course…'-the rituals of young Mods of the period with such panache and punch.

One of the great Jam riffs and one of the great narratives of the young ideal-perfectly capturing both the ups and downs, the highs and lows of being young and being alive in fact !

'…Saturday's boys live life with insults,
Drink lots of beer and wait for half time results,
Afternoon tea in the light-a-bite, chat up the girls, they Dig it!
Saturday's girls work in Tesco's and Woolworths,
Wear cheap perfume cause it's all they can afford,
Go to discos they drink baby cham talk to Jan, in bingo
accents.

Saturday's kids play one arm bandits,
They never win but that's not the point is it,
Dip in silver paper when their pints go flat,
How about that, far out!

Their mums and dads smoke capstan non filters,
Wallpaper lives cause they all die of cancer,
What goes on, what goes wrong.
Save up their money for a holiday,

To Selsey bill or Bracklesham bay,
Think about the future, when they'll settle down,
Marry the girl next door, with one on the way.

These are the real creatures that time has forgot,
Not given a thought, it's the system,
Hate the system, what's the system?

Saturday's kids live in council houses,
Wear V-necked shirts and baggy trousers,
Drive cortinas fur trimmed dash boards,
Stains on the seats - in the back of course !...'

Working class poetry that groups like Madness and the Smiths were to also explore-
making the mundane extraordinary in fact.

Always a crowd pleaser and delivered to great effect as a trio, firmly establishing
Weller's place as the Working Class Poet Laureate of this period.

For me especially poignant, for even now when I hear the opening bars I am transported
to those dank London streets of the late Nineteen Seventies and all those memories come
flooding back-fondly I must add-thank you Paul !

33. Pretty Green

For me 'Sound Affects' remains the Jam's finest album and certainly one of the greatest British LPs, up there with the leading discs from such luminaries as the Beatles, Bowie and Radiohead (yes, Radiohead-'Moon shaped Pool' is genius), and it cracks off with the mercurial 'Pretty Green'; once again Weller capturing the mood of the period and the rampant glorification of Capitalism in the hands of Thatcher the Butcher of Grantham and the adoration of money for money's sake.

Foxton's bass signally ominously the pessimism of the song and the sense of foreboding-certainly the pervasive influence of the Gang of Four at hand, as well as the musical intricacies of Wire are evident but as always with Weller he always retains that sense of melody and rhythm, never belying his Beatlesque roots.

Stunning live, the song catches fire as it complements the three-piece perfectly: Weller's jagged discordant notes, the throb of Foxton's bass, and Bucklers criminally underrated drumming.

'...I've got a pocket full of pretty green
I'm gonna put it in the fruit machine
I'm gonna put it in the jukebox
It's gonna play all the records in the hit parade

This is the pretty green, this is society
You can't do nothing, unless it's in the pocket
Oh no

I've got a pocket full of pretty green

I'm gonna give it to the man behind the counter
He's gonna give me food and water
I'm gonna eat that and look for more

And they didn't teach me that in school
It's something that I learnt on my own
That power is measured by the pound or the fist
It's as clear as this oh

I've got a pocket full of pretty green!...'

Lyrically so apt, astute and indeed nothing ever changes.

Remains one of the Jam classics and the themes of consumerism and capitalism and the power that only the elite possess have been mainstays throughout his career and have remained to this day.

Certainly reminding us of his working class upbringing and also that times were hard-and millions indeed still suffer.

34. Monday

Paul Weller is quite rightly regarded as a great balladeer now and there were nascent signs during the Jam period to suggest indeed what was to come ,and 'Monday' is one of the finest Weller songs from the period.

Fitting snugly between the power of 'Pretty Green' and the pop brilliance of 'But I'm different now' it's one of the most beautiful of Weller's melodies and his great love songs-it's pure Mod as it portrays the prosaic nature of love for young lovers.

'…Rainclouds came and stole my thunder
Left me barren like a desert
But a sunshine girl like you
It's worth going through
I will never be embarrassed about love again

Tortured winds that blew me over
When I start to think that I'm something special
They tell me that I'm not
And they're right and I'm glad and I'm not
I will never be embarrassed about that again.

Oh baby I'm dreaming of Monday,
Oh baby will I see you again
Oh baby I'm dreaming of Monday…'

The poetic images he seemed to be taking in reflecting a part of his youthful development.

Certainly Beatlesque in sound and would not have been out of place on the Revolver or Rubber Soul LPs.

McCartneyesque with a touch of 'Tommyesque Townshend Who' thrown in for good measure.

Another underrated song in the Weller canon, and a harbinger of the even greater things to come throughout the rest of his career.

35. But I'm different now

Weller has always had an ear for a great musical riff ,no better evidenced on this corker from 'Sound Affects'-blistering guitar, allied with great backing from Foxton's bass and the drive of Buckler's drums makes this one of the lesser known Jam classics.

Almost a perfect fusion of the Beatlesque pop sensibility, the modernism of the Who, and laced with the cutting edge of punk power : it's pure pop at it's very best.

Lyrically an offbeat love song demonstrating Weller's confidence in his song writing during what was to be arguably his greatest period-culminating in the 'Gift' set which also displayed his versatility.

'…Picked you up and let you down and
I never said a word
But I'm different now and I'm glad that you're my girl

Mess you 'round and upset you
I hurt you most of all
But I'm different now and I'm glad that you're my girl

Fun lasts for seconds, love lasts for days but
But you can't have both
And I'm different now but I'm glad that you're my girl

Because I know I done some things
That I should never have done
But I'm different now and I'm glad that you're my girl…'

The cocky power pop, pure Mod-pure Jimmy Quadrophenia.

Beautifully placed too on the 'Sound Affects' set between the melodic 'Monday 'and the muscular 'Set the House Ablaze', one of the perfect Jam songs and one of Weller's finest moments- not the disposable 3 minute pop many think it is at first listen.

36. Start

Weller's bravura confidence in his own writing and the consummate musicianship of the band is perhaps best exemplified in the excellent 'Start'; yes, it acknowledges a huge debt to Taxman from the wonderful 'Revolver', albeit a pastiche of everything Beatlesque around that Revolver period; the pulsating bassline purloined from McCartney (a Weller hero), the lyrical preoccupations of isolation, transience made plain.

'...It's not important for you to know my name
Nor I to know yours
If we communicate for two minutes only
It will be enough

For knowing that someone in this world
Feels as desperate as me
And what you give is what you get.
It doesn't matter if we never meet again,
What we have said will always remain.

If we get through for two minutes only,
It will be a start!

For knowing that someone in this life,
Loves with a passion called hate
And what you give is what you get.

If I never ever see you
If I never ever see you
If I never ever see you - again.

And what you give is what you get!...'

One of the great Jam singles, and of course the video being homage to the Psychedelic of the Nineteen Sixties showing the band at their very height of greatness.

The song sits between 'Set the House Ablaze' and 'That's Entertainment' on the magnificent 'Sound Affects' album, and demonstrates both the flexibility and the ingenuity of the band as a tight unit, evidencing Weller's recent claim as to how electrifying the band were live and on vinyl-the song became a fantastic live favourite and indeed Weller has played it live in recent slot sets rolling back the years-the quality of the song remains and it has become a timeless classic, still sounding as fresh as it was on its release-quite an achievement.

37. That's Entertainment

If you want to highlight perhaps the greatest song in the Weller repertoire, one which illustrated at such an early stage his quality-his 'Waterloo Sunset' moment as it were-as well as a song which exemplifies his wonderful lyricism which has such a poetic and timeless quality then it must be 'That's Entertainment'.

Sheepishly hidden away on' Sound Affects', while released in Europe initially as a single which made its way into the English Charts as an import, it remains one of the most perfect pop songs of any era, transcending classification and musical boundaries.

Political with a small 'p',one of the key songs of that time summarising the bleakness and sterility of the period but also emphasizing the sounds of teenage years : first forays into the world of love, the ennui of life on the estates of mainland Britain : the smash of glass and the rumble of boots indeed.

'…A police car and a screaming siren
A pneumatic drill and ripped up concrete
A baby wailing and stray dog howling
The screech of brakes and lamp light blinking

That's entertainment,
 that's entertainment

A smash of glass and a rumble of boots
An electric train and a ripped up 'phone booth
Paint splattered walls and the cry of a tomcat
Lights going out and a kick in the balls

That's entertainment,
that's entertainment
Days of speed and slow time Mondays

Pissing down with rain on a boring Wednesday
Watching the news and not eating your tea
A freezing cold flat and damp on the walls

That's entertainment,
that's entertainment

Waking up at six am on a cool warm morning
Opening the windows and breathing in petrol
An amateur band rehearsing in a nearby yard
Watching the tele and thinking about your holidays

That's entertainment,
that's entertainment

Waking up from bad dreams and smoking cigarettes
Cuddling a warm girl and smelling stale perfume
A hot summer's day and sticky black tarmac
Feeding ducks in the park and wishing you were far away

That's entertainment,
that's entertainment

Two lovers kissing amongst the scream of midnight
Two lovers missing the tranquillity of solitude
Getting a cab and travelling on buses
Reading the graffiti about slashed seat affairs

That's entertainment,
That's entertainment...'

One of the most eloquent of anti-Thatcher tirades, prescient of the havoc she would
wreak upon the poorest in the county before they were promised fame and fortune in the
get rich, borrow money HP culture that ensued from that period onwards.

Weller has revisited the song live in his solo shows to great effect and it has always stood
out as poignant and powerful-that's entertainment indeed!

38. Dream Time

One of my abiding memories of the Jam shows from late 1980 was the apocalyptic force of 'Dream Time' knocking us senseless with sheer joy and passion ; it's force was such it threw us one way and another, the sea of bodies often reducing an auditorium to ruins-the Rainbow and Hammersmith concerts were especial highlights here-and it was a perfect summation of what the Jam had so successfully achieved by this stage ; it had the force and aggression of punk and I've often wondered how the wonderful Joe Strummer would have sounded singing this-and was once again a wonderful example of Weller's eloquence and lyricism.

'...Streets I ran, this whole town
Backstreet's and all, I wanted to leave there
But no matter how fast I ran, my feet were glued
I just couldn't move there
I saw the hate and lots of people
I heard my name called above the noise
I tried to speak but my tongue was tied
Bumped into emptiness and started to cry, oh no

[Chorus:]I saw the lights and the pretty girls
And I thought to myself what a pretty world
But there's something else here that puts me off
And I'm so scared dear, my love comes in frozen packs
Bought in a supermarket

Streets I ran, through wind and rain,
Around this place amongst streaming sunshine.
Scared I was, sweating now.
Feeling of doom, my bowels turned to water
I felt hot breath whisper in my ear
I looked for somewhere to hide but every where's closed

I shut my eyes pretend not to be here
This feelings much to real to ever disappear, oh no

[Chorus]And I'm so scared dear
My love comes in frozen packs…'

Existential dread no less, the anomie experienced in modern societies ;a real depth to Weller's writing and 'Dream Time' encapsulates Weller's preoccupations with an individual's place in society and the predicaments we face and the stresses and concerns we have to endure.

A Modernist nightmare.

Surely this must be one of Pete Townshend's favourite Jam songs given his concern with the plight of individuals in society.

One of the most underrated and least regarded Jam tracks and surely due a critical re-evaluation.

39. Liza Radley

Such was the quality of the Jam songbook from 78-81 and the potency of Weller's song writing itself that many classics were hidden away on albums or secreted on B Sides, such was the case with 'Liza Radley', the reverse of the stunning Start single.

Clearly redolent of McCartney's melodious side as well as possessing the wistfulness of Ray Davies; it's a beautiful, a profoundly English, Modernist love song, with a literary prowess with echoes of Austen and Lawrence as well as a poetic sensibility.

'...Liza Radley, see the girl with long hair
See her creeping 'cross summer lawns at midnight
And all the people in the town where we live say
she's not quite right
She don't fit in with a small town

They just can't understand why she's doesn't stay in hospital
In a darkened room it's for their lives only she cries
Liza Radley, see her jump through loneliness
Liza Radley, take me when you go

And as the people pass by, their heads in the air
On to with their life's, she records a lonely sigh,
But no matter what they say, in her mind she knows,
Their dream of life they won't never find

And all the people in the town where we live say
she's not quite right
She don't fit in with a small town
They just can't understand she's doesn't stay in hospital
In a darkened room it's for their lives only she cries.

Liza Radley, I pledge myself to you alone.
But she kissed my face and said
Love means nothing at all

She kissed my face and said
Life means nothing at all...'

On any level this is one of Weller's great love songs of the period : beautiful melody, great lyrics and a band in perfect tune.

Arguably it would have sat perfectly on side 2 'Sound Affects'-but that's a little personal gripe-but it has been woefully undervalued and ignored.

It's for me also a great influence on the early work of the Britpoppers especially Blur,OCS and Oasis-and could easily be covered by an Ed Sheeran,Jake Bugg etc-one to be revisited and in real need of critical reassessment and revaluation.

40. Happy Together

After the perfection of the Sound Affects set it did appear impossible for the Jam to repeat this magnificent musical success, and indeed the 'Gift' is a mighty fine record and in some ways the transition record between Weller's abandonment of the Rock,Pop,Mod perfection and his embracing of the new vision of old school R and B,Soul,a Funk infused sound which was of course was to find its embodiment in the Style Council in later years.

'Happy Together' sits nicely between these two era's : the now familiar Weller power pop chords, blasting away through a beautiful melody, and encapsulating what at that time what you wold describe as the Jam sound : a bit of Mod,Traffic,with a punk ethic.

A fabulous curtain raiser for the Gift album and a great track live which complemented the Jam strength as a trio.

How ironic given this was the last Jam album and Weller simultaneously was pondering disbanding the group and with this very much lodged in his consciousness this may have be a Freudian Slip on his part?-they were not happy together after all ?

'...Thought that I would forget you?
Heaven knows that's not my style.
And that I would let you.
Walk away without at least goodbye.

You shouldn't let those feelings fool you.
You shouldn't let those feelings get you down.

We're happy together now.
Feeling you close to me baby.
Happy 'til the end of time.
We're happy together now.

Feeling you close to me baby.
Happy `til the end of time.

We're happy together.. happy together.

Thought that I was a devil?
But I'm an angel waiting for my wings
And I was out to hurt you?
But I've no wish to ever cause you pain.
`Cause there's enough in this world of sorrow.
I've no wish to add some more to it.

We're happy together now.
Feeling you close to me baby.
Happy till the end of time.
We're happy together now.

Feeling you close to me baby.
Happy till the end of time.
We're happy together.. happy together.

I don't hear a symphony
all I hear is the beating of...
what I'm trying to say is you're my only.

We're happy together now.
Feeling you close to me baby.
Happy till the end of time.
We're happy together now.

Feeling you close to me baby.
Happy till the end of time.

We're happy together.. happy together NOW !...'

Probably wishful thinking at the time but a great Jam song nonetheless.

41. Running on the Spot

There's a lot to admire on the 'Gift' album but it was almost impossible for Weller and the Jam to surpass the perfection of 'Sound Affects' and 1980 in general with the wondrous 'Going Underground' and 'Start' singles but this is certainly one of the stand out stabs at doing so and one of the best sets of lyrics penned by Weller.

Typically robust three piece sound now honed to perfection in complete control, and with great power .'Running on the spot' is a fascinating track for a number of reasons : lyrically Weller resistant to becoming that spokesman for a generation is all too evident (although many have been correct in seeing him rather than Strummer as the shaper of young political opinions, forays into literature etc.-well he certainly was for me !),as he correctly surmises are we making any real progress at all, are we just kidding themselves, existentially lost in modern society.

'...I was hoping we'd make real progress
But it seems we have lost the power
Any tiny step of advancement
Is like a raindrop falling into the ocean

We're running on the spot - always have - always will?
We're just the next generation of the emotionally crippled.

Though we keep piling up the building blocks
The structure never seems to get any higher
Because we keep kicking out the foundations
And stand useless while our lives fall down.

I believe in life - and I believe in love
But the world in which I live in - keeps trying to prove me wrong.

Out in the pastures we call society

You can't see further than the bottom of your glass
Only young but easily shocked
You get all violent when the boat gets rocked

Just like sheep - little lambs into the slaughter
Don't fully grasp what exactly is wrong
Truth is you never cared - still
You get all violent when the boat gets rocked

Intelligence should be our first weapon
And stop revelling in rejection
And follow yourselves, not some ageing drain brain
Whose quite content to go on feeding you garbage

We're running on the spot - always have - always will?
We're just the next generation of the emotionally crippled…'

If musically not a sonic boom, one of the last great Jam power pop exercises
demonstrating the band at its very best.

Could this also subconsciously perhaps be indicative of Weller's state of mind when
deciding to dissolve the Jam-were they also in danger of running on the spot-something
Weller had also insisted he and Jam were never going to do.

42. Carnation

It was fitting that this song remains a favourite of the Gallagher brothers and indeed Liam has performed this song on a number of occasions –it's causticity,bile,brooding quality suits the world weary vocal style of the Britpop community and it certainly still stands the test of time and for me still remains the finest Weller song on the Gift perfectly demonstrating the lyrical range and depth of his writing.

As Weller developed his style he became more confessional over the years, love songs became more diffuse, more difficult as he talked about his phlegmatism,his frosty side emotionally, his shyness-he has always been very insular and inexpressive emotionally (he has a grapefruit manner indeed as he later confided on' Peacock Suit') and this really is one of Weller's finest sets of lyrics.

'...If you gave me a fresh carnation
I would only crush its tender petals
With me you'll have no escape
And at the same time there'll be nowhere to settle

I trample down all life in my wake
I eat it up and take the cake
I just avert my eyes to the pain
Of someone's loss helping my gain

If you gave me a dream for my pocket
You'd be plugging in the wrong socket
With me there's no room for the future
With me there's no room with a view at all

I am out of season all year 'round
Hear machinery roar to my empty sound
Touch my heart and feel winter

Hold my hand and be doomed forever

If you gave me a fresh carnation
I would only crush its tender petals
With me you'll have no escape
And at the same time there'll be nowhere to settle.

And if you're wondering by now who I am
Look no further than the mirror
Because I am the Greed and Fear
And every ounce of Hate in you...'

Especially powerful live, and one that captured the Jam as a unit musically, a powerful piece that packs a punch-I'm certain it's a big hit awaiting a great cover version-imagine it being sung by an Adele or Sam Smith and you'll see the quality of the song itself.

Another underrated Weller classic.

43. A Town called Malice

It's always interesting whenever urban gritty dramas from the 1980s feature or indeed films highlighting the decade, this more than any other song of the period features in all its glory; understandably one of the most recognised Jam classics and a key part of the Weller legacy.

It's also an important song in the Weller canon for a number of other reasons : firstly, it represents the first transition in Jam sound towards the inevitability of the Style Council, trumpeting its Northern Soul,R and B soul, proudly from that unmistakeable Foxton bass line intro through to the modernist keyboards and pulsating percussion ; secondly, quite simply it remains one of the great songs of the inter Thatcher period with the ravages of many cities ,the heartlessness of Politics at the time and the inhumanity of the period despite the celebration of the get rich culture; and thirdly, it's arguably the last great Jam 45 (admittedly there were great songs to come) but this seemed to represent the height of the Jams grandeur.

'…Better stop dreaming of the quiet life
Cause it's the one we'll never know
And quit running for that runaway bus
Cause those rosy days are few
And, stop apologizing for the things you've never done,
Cause time is short and life is cruel
But it's up to us to change
This town called malice.

Rows and rows of disused milk floats
Stand dying in the dairy yard
And a hundred lonely housewives clutch empty milk
Bottles to their hearts
Hanging out their old love letters on the line to dry
It's enough to make you stop believing when tears come

Fast and furious
In a town called malice.

Struggle after struggle, year after year
The atmosphere's a fine blend of ice
I'm almost stone cold dead
In a town called malice.

A whole street's belief in Sunday's roast beef
Gets dashed against the Co-op
To either cut down on beer or the kids new gear
It's a big decision in a town called malice.

The ghost of a steam train, echoes down my track
It's at the moment bound for nowhere
Just going round and round
Playground kids and creaking swings
Lost laughter in the breeze
I could go on for hours and I probably will
But I'd sooner put some joy back
In this town called malice…'

Always thunderous live not only as a Jam classic, it's often cropped up in Weller's live
solo set-it remains a durable quality state of Weller rage-still striking when played today;
and a perfect summary of 1980s Britain.

44. Funeral Pyre

I have no doubt that the one Jam single most people-not aficionados of course-would neglect to mention is the magnificent, Wagnerian 'Funeral Pyre'; check the stylist Weller in the atmospheric video too on You tube if you can-Weller is the epitome of cool looking like a Stevie Marriott a la 1967 in a magnificent full length black suede jacket (or something similar!).

A towering, thunderous record ,propelled by a pulsating bass line and the spiralling, anarchic guitar which had touches of the Gang of Four, the Clash, even the Slits, but remaining quintessentially the Jam at the height of their powers.

Lyricaly,once again Weller rails at the state, it's control,censorship,and establishment per se-and the seeming futility of resistance against the status quo and rebelling-also depicting the dangers of dictatorship and the absolute power it brings-no doubt a reference to the ever darker and dominant Thatcherism of the time that was repressing the poorest under the malevolent Margret Thatcher, seeing the persecution of the poor and the needy while those in power, got stronger, eviscerating the poor.

'...Down in amongst the streets tonight
Books will burn, people laugh and cry in their turmoil
(Turmoil turns rejoiceful)
Shed your fears and lose your guilt
Tonight we burn responsibility in the fire
We'll watch the flames grow higher!
But if you get too burnt, you can't come back home

And as I was standing by the edge
I could see the faces of those led pissing themselves laughing
(And the flames grew)
Their mad eyes bulged their flushed faces said
The weak get crushed as the strong grow stronger

We feast on flesh and drink on blood
Live by fear and despise love in a crises
(What with today's high prices)

Bring some paper and bring some wood
Bring what's left of all your love for the fire
We'll watch the flames grow higher!

But if you get too burnt - you can't come back home
And as I was standing by the edge
I could see the faces of those led pissing themselves laughing
(And the flames grew)

Their mad eyes bulged their flushed faces said
The weak get crushed as the strong grow stronger
In the funeral pyre

We'll watch the flames grow higher
But if you get too burnt - you can't come back home
(Well I feel so old, when I feel so young
Well I just can't grow up to meet the demands)…'

One of the lost great Jam singles-and once again solely over looked.

45. Above the Clouds

If any track marked the transition point between the Soulified modernism of the Style Council and the emergence of the reborn Paul Weller, it's 'Above the Clouds' which has proud place on the wonderful first Paul Weller solo record which is surely due re-evaluation.

A beautiful lilting summer sound exemplifying Weller's soul boy credentials with his songwriting prowess ;once again with a large amount of Weller's output it deserves covering by anybody with a strong enough voice to carry it off-a Lianne la Havas comes to mind as does the more obvious Adele-and it would be a guaranteed major hit-even Olly Murs might do this justice.

'…Autumn blew its leaves at me,
Threatening winter as I walked.

Summer always goes so quick,
Barely stopping like my thoughts.

Which dip and spin and change so fast
I have to wonder - Will I last.
Through the windows of the train,
I caught reflections of a paper cup,
Hanging small in a pale blue sky,
Never knowing which way's up.

Above the clouds, what's to be found,
I have to wonder - Will I be around.

As my anger shouts - At my own self-doubt,
So a sadness creeps - Into my dreams
When you're scared of living - But afraid to die

I get scared of giving - And I must find the faith to beat it
I must be me that's rushing by,
Time just lingers on the wind.

Bristling' through my open fears,
I wonder what it's going to bring.
Above the clouds, what's to be found,
I have to wonder - Will I be around.

Run and hide, run and hide
I catch the sail at evening's tide…'

Musically, perfectly Mod in execution-coming alive like an old R and B standard covered by a Stevie Marriott Small Faces Unit.

Great live too, and fits seamlessly into any of his live setl lists as an exemplar of the quality of is songbook.

I often revisit the first album and always remain surprised by the depth and the contemporaneity of the sound.

46. Out of the Sinking

I would wager that this wonderful Weller solo single sits well and truly in his own top ten of songs, as it crystallizes so well the key influences in both enabling him to fuse his own style and why he has always remained so commercially viable and culturally 'cool'; the sound of a tight Small Faces unit, suffused with an almost Mayfield/Impressions like R and B sensibility, and of course updated with a rock/punkish punch and power that highlights how Weller is almost always at his best when he sings with a punch and conviction and positively spits his lyrics out with a venom unmatched.

'…Past midnight's hold

Where the world's awaiting

I'll wait for you love

But I close my eyes, as there's pain too in paradise

Hey baby say - just what you're thinking

Know I know it - yeh, feel I'm sinking

Know I feel it - I know you feel it too

Across the water, there's a boat that

Will take us away

It is shining for me

All I need to be

But I can't find the key

The one to make me believe

Late at night
When the world is dreaming
Way past the stars

That ignore our fate & all twinkle too late to save us
So we save ourselves…'

A great song played live it always takes me back to the Feelgoods brand of Pub Rock too in a positive sense as it 'rock and rolls ' live and possesses a power that hits home every time.

Surely one of the greatest singles in the Weller canon and as with so much of his output-due to the size of his body of work-often overlooked-but we in the fraternity know how good this track is!!!!

47. From the Floorboards up

I'm always reminded of Noel Gallagher's observation that the track represented Weller getting his Mojo back fully intact as it ripped through the airwaves-the strident power chords disorientating us, a searing power pop blast that took us all back to the early 80's but also certainly proving to be a signature tune for the way ahead for Weller and the amazing burst of creativity which was to follow.

There are the obvious nods to the past here: Weller's love of the Feel good's and especially the guitar playing of the wonderful Wilco Johnson, as well as the fusion of early Jam, the Gang of Four/Wire, early Who even-sure one of the great contemporary mod classics and a floor filler at that.

'...I've got a feeling
From the floorboards up
Call it a calling
If you like that touch
Call it what you will
I really don't care too much

I've got a feeling
And I know it's right
I get it most evenings
If not every night
It sings in the air
And dances like candle light

When we play, we play, we play
Mama, from the floorboards up
When we dance, we dance, we dance
Papa, from the floorboards up
When we sway, we sway as one
From the floorboards up

From the floorboards up

I get a feeling
From the walls and chairs
They tell me of the things that
Have always been there
And all that is not
Will have to go back to dust

When we play, we play, we play
Mama, from the floorboards up
When we dance, we dance, we dance
Papa, from the floorboards up
When we sway, we sway as one
From the floorboards up
From the floorboards up

I've got a feeling
And I know it's right
I get it most evenings
If not every night
It sings in the air
And dances like candle light

When we play, we play, we play
Mama, from the floorboards up
When we dance, we dance, we dance
Daddy, from the floorboards up
When we sway, we sway as one
From the floorboards up
From the floorboards up
From the floorboards up...'

It sounded as if Weller needed to reacquaint himself with his roots and go back to basics I order to propel himself forward again as he has done so with such aplomb, witness the near perfect succession of albums that followed.

One of the greatest live Weller songs, it never fails to ignite and remind us how good he really is-always needing to shake himself up, dust himself off,and bloom again-a fantastic slab of rock/pop brilliance.

48. Hung up

One of the key songs in the Weller solo canon is 'Hung up' and for me one of his most innovative and challenging singles-innovative in the sense of musically wonderfully meshing the acoustic sounds and the rock elements in one momentous track, and challenging as Weller's lyrics are once again almost existentially summarise his preoccupation with 'self' and the moments of self-doubt, depression and disillusionment that can be so destructive in all of our lives.

'…Hidden in the back seat of my head
Some place I can't remember where
I found it just by coincidence
An' now I'm all hung up again
Just like a soldier from the past
Who won't be told it's over yet
Refusing to put down his gun
He's gotta hurt someone
He'll keep on fighting 'til his war is won

Waiting for the moment
Keep on looking for a sign

Extraordinary, trying to cease the war inside
Hidden in the back seat of my head
Some place I can't remember where
I found it just by coincidence
An' now I'm all hung up again…'

A favourite of both Blur and Oasis and in a way show's them how to do it-a perfect exercise in producing a near perfect pop single, something which appears to have been lost currently-it also reminds one lyrically of Townshend and one can imagine Roger Daltry doing this song justice too as part of either the Quadrophenia or Tommy sets.

Also great when played live possessing a real power while also always being thoughtful and provocative.

Certainly due to critical re-evaluation and merits a considered 'cover' as it still sounds so contemporary and powerful.

49. Speak like a child

Many will be surprised by my choice here, the first Style Council single (and I do apologise for my neglect of a number of Style Council classics-see my introduction once again!!!).

'Speak like a child' is a great pop song full stop and a hugely influential one as it was so radical at the time: the fire and skill of the Jam was replaced by this rampantly commercial R and B, soulified pop record welcoming his new view of the world and indeed of himself-it was such a brave step at the time.

'...Your hair hangs in golden steps
You're a bonafide in every respect
You are walking through streets that mean nothing to you

You believe you're above it and I don't really blame you
Maybe that's why you speak like a child;
The things you're saying like "I'm so free and so wild"
And I believe it when you look in my eyes;
You offer me a life, and never lies
Least only the kind to make me smile
Your clothes are clean and your mind is productive
It shops in store where only the best buy
You're cool and hard, and if I sound like a lecher
It's probably true,
But at least there's no lecture
I really like it when you speak like a child
The crazy sayings like "I'm so free and so wild"
You have to make a bargain with me now
A promise that you won't change somehow
No way, now how
Spent all day thinking about you
Spent all night coming to terms with it
Time and conditions are built to tame

Nothing lasts with age, so people say
But I will always try to feel the same
I really like it when you speak like a child
I really like it when you speak like a child
The way you hate the homely rank and the file
The way you're so proud to be oh, so free and so wild
I really like it when you speak like a child
I really like it when you speak like a child
I really like it when you speak like a child
The way you're so proud to be oh, so free and so wild...'

I remembered being so floored initially missing the power of the Jam as a three piece
powerhouse and poetry/passion of the lyrics, but on reflection what a marvellous pop
single, and in many senses the quintessential Style Council record: beautifully crafted,
timeless, which could have graced the charts (either mainstream or Soul) at any time
between 1960-1985-surely the test of a quality single.

One of the watershed moments for me was the watching the Style Council play this live
on Top of the Pops, introducing Weller's new vision to the public, and genuinely taking a
risk which he has always done-much to his credit-throughout his career.

50. Walls come tumbling down

The 1980's was a highly political era with the pernicious Thatcherism, unemployment at an all-time high, the proliferation of nuclear weapons as well as the worldwide nuclear threat itself, and Weller had seemed so politically relevant with the later Jam classics but he also ensured that rather like a Curtis Mayfield politically infused Impressions he used the Style Council to express political ideas within this period and nowhere more joyously, powerfully and stridently than in the magnificent 'Walls come tumbling down'-in many respects this is also a perfect encapsulation of Weller's thoughts throughout his career : it has the fire and fury of the Jam, the depth and passion of his solo work as well as the beautiful melodic sense of the Style Council-all in one cracking sparkling Style Council single.

'…You don't have to take this crap
You don't have to sit back and relax
You can actually try changing it

I know we've always been taught to rely
Upon those in authority
But you never know until you try
How things just might be
If we came together so strongly
Are you gonna try to make this work
Or spend your days down in the dirt

You see things can change
YES an' walls can come tumbling down!

Governments crack and systems fall
'cause Unity is powerful
Lights go out - walls come tumbling down!

The competition is a colour TV

We're on still pause with the video machine
That keep you slave to the H.P.
Until the Unity is threatend by
Those who have and who have not
Those who are with and those who are without
And dangle jobs like a donkey's carrot
Until you don't know where you are
Are you gonna realize
The class war's real and not mythologized
And like Jericho - You see walls can come tumbling down!

Down! You'll be too weak to fight it
Down! Ah, the world's ignited
Down! Oh, when you're united
Are you gonna be threatend by
The public enemies No. 10
Those who play the power game
They take the profits - you take the blame
When they tell you there's no rise in pay
Are you gonna try an' make this work
Or spend your days down in the dirt
You see things CAN change
YES an' walls can come tumbling down…'

Unity is indeed powerful and Weller's well documented support for Red Wedge and the rebellion against the severity and heartlessness of Thatcherism is all too evident-and please note Weller's recent declaration that he will be doing what he can to support the new Labour Leader Jeremy Corbyn .

The biggest tribute I can pay is that any time I revisit this track I think of the late great Marvin Gaye or Curtis Mayfield getting to grips with this, one of Weller's greatest songs-and one that lives long in the memory.

Printed in Great Britain
by Amazon